YALDING

Please return on or before the latest date above.
You can renew online at *www.kent.gov.uk/libs*
or by telephone 08458 247 200

507. 8

CHARTER MARK

CUSTOMER SERVICE EXCELLENCE

Libraries & Archives

Kent
County
Council

LIB 7

D1427360

Visit Nick Arnold at
www.nickarnold-website.com

Thanks to the students of Cramlington Community High School who came up with the nettle soup idea.

Scholastic Children's Books,
Euston House, 24 Eversholt Street,
London, NW1 1DB, UK

A division of Scholastic Ltd
London ~ New York ~ Toronto ~ Sydney ~ Auckland
Mexico City ~ New Delhi ~ Hong Kong

First published in the UK by Scholastic Ltd, 2007

Text copyright © Nick Arnold, 2007
Cover illustration © Tony De Saulles, 2007
Inside illustrations by Dave Smith, based on the style of the original
Horrible Science artwork by Tony De Saulles
Illustrations © Dave Smith, 2007
Colour by Tom Connell
All rights reserved

10 digit ISBN 0 439 94408 2
13 digit ISBN 978 0439944 08 3

Printed and bound by Tien Wah Press Pte. Ltd, Malaysia

2 4 6 8 10 9 7 5 3 1

The right of Nick Arnold, Tony De Saulles and Dave Smith to be identified as the author and
illustrators of this work respectively has been asserted by them in accordance with the Copyright,
Designs and Patents Act, 1988.

CONTENTS

INTRODUCTION

Mealtimes can be miserable – especially if your parents won't let you talk at the table and force you to chew every mouthful 144 times.

But that doesn't mean food can't be fun. This Horrible Handbook is designed to help you become a horrible scientist. It's full of foul food experiments – and that gives you the perfect parent-proof excuse for anti-social activities such as cooking revolting recipes and creating kitchen chaos. If anyone tells you off you can simply say:

> BUT IT'S ALL IN THE CAUSE OF SCIENCE!

In other words – Horrible Science! So what are you waiting for? Why not try a few evil experiments and freak your family with foul food facts?

And whatever you do, I bet your mealtimes will never be the same again!

SICKENING STARTERS

Ready to start your training as a horrible scientist? Great – we'll get started as we've met a person who's itching to meet us. (He's itching because his dog's got fleas.) He's a money-grabbing New York private eye by the name of M I Gutzache…

I NEED THE DOLLARS. THAT DOG OF MINE EATS MONEY!

We've teamed him up with Horrible Science expert Professor N Large in order to test the experiments…

I DON'T KNOW WHY YOU BROUGHT THAT MISERABLE MOGGIE!

BUT TIDDLES IS MY FRIEND!

OK LET'S GET STARTED – I'VE GOT BILLS TO PAY!

NOT SO FAST GUTZACHE – YOU HAVEN'T READ THE RULES YET…

IT'S ONLY PAGE 6 AND THEY'RE ALREADY ARGUING!

RULES
FOR TRAINEE HORRIBLE SCIENTISTS

1 ALWAYS READ THE EXPERIMENT BEFORE YOU TRY IT.
Make sure you have every item of equipment.
Here are some essential items...

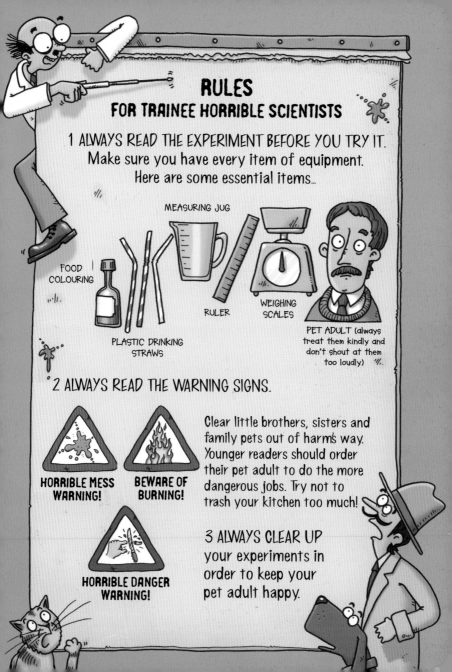

MEASURING JUG

FOOD COLOURING

RULER

WEIGHING SCALES

PLASTIC DRINKING STRAWS

PET ADULT (always treat them kindly and don't shout at them too loudly)

2 ALWAYS READ THE WARNING SIGNS.

HORRIBLE MESS WARNING!

BEWARE OF BURNING!

HORRIBLE DANGER WARNING!

Clear little brothers, sisters and family pets out of harm's way. Younger readers should order their pet adult to do the more dangerous jobs. Try not to trash your kitchen too much!

3 ALWAYS CLEAR UP your experiments in order to keep your pet adult happy.

SO WHEN DO WE START?

NOT UNTIL YOU'VE READ THESE SCIENCE FACTS!

Science facts to remember...

ATOMS – tiny balls of matter that make up every substance in the universe (including you).

MOLECULE – a group of atoms joined together.

Atoms and molecules can bond together or separate in CHEMICAL REACTIONS.

YAWN

YAWN

RAISING RICE BALLS

WHAT YOU NEED:
- 18–20-cm-tall jar with 400 g of rice
- Large bowl • Lightweight ball 3 cm across –
a table-tennis ball is ideal • A similar-sized rubber ball
- Metal ball or similar-sized pebble

WHAT YOU DO:

1 Place the light ball in the jar and pour the rice over it.

2 Shake the jar.

PUT THE LID ON FIRST!!!

3 Now empty all the rice into the bowl and remove the ball.

4 Repeat steps 1 to 3 using the rubber ball and then the metal ball.

YOU SHOULD FIND:

You might think that the lighter ball will "float" to the top of the rice and the heavier balls will stay at the bottom. But in fact ALL of the balls float.

So what's going on?

THIS IS BECAUSE:

As you shake the rice, some of the grains slip under the ball and begin to lift it. Even the heaviest ball is lifted higher and higher until it pops up on top of the rice.

Bet you never knew!

Rice can be used to make concrete. And no – I'm not talking about your dad's burnt rice pudding setting like concrete. In some countries rice-seed cases are actually used to strengthen concrete.

ALIEN DOUGH
MONSTERS

WHAT YOU NEED:

- 100 g of salt
- 100 g of flour
- Measuring jug
- Glass with 100 ml water
- Green food colouring
- Bowl
- Wooden spoon
- Weighing scales
- Teaspoon
- Cream of tartar
- Saucepan
- Dish
- A grisly imagination
- Your trusty pet adult

HORRIBLE MESS!

Food colouring features a lot in this book. It can stain clothes and hands so wear old clothes and be careful – this is your one and only warning!

WHAT YOU DO:

1 Order your pet adult to heat the cooker to 100–120°C.

2 Measure the salt and flour into the bowl. Add 4 heaped teaspoonfuls of cream of tartar and mix well.

3 Mix 30 drops of food colouring in the glass of water.

4 Add the coloured water to the mixture in the bowl and stir it into a gruesome gunky green gloop.

5 Spoon the gloop into the saucepan. Place the saucepan on the cooker and stir the mixture until it turns into a thick dough.

BEWARE OF BURNING!

Younger readers will need adult help.

6 Turn your dough on to the dish and leave it to cool for 15 minutes.

SPLAT

SQUELCH!

YOU SHOULD FIND:
You can make the dough into a really revolting space monster.

But whatever you do DON'T EAT IT! It tastes really bad! (even worse than a real space monster).

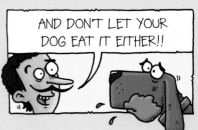

AND DON'T LET YOUR DOG EAT IT EITHER!!

THIS IS BECAUSE:

Flour contains molecules called proteins. Your body needs proteins to grow and repair itself. Flour contains a protein called gluten, and that's what makes a stringy mess when you mix flour and water. Salt is made up of sodium-chloride molecules that rip the gluten apart in a nasty way and the cream of tartar helps to puff the dough out – so the dough becomes softer and lighter and easier to shape.

Bet you never knew!

If you want to sound like a scientist you can call cream of tartar by its scientific name – potassium hydrogen tartrate. It's actually made by mixing tartaric acid (taken from mashed-up grapes left over from winemaking) with potassium hydroxide. This second chemical is used for dissolving warts and cleaning false teeth.

BASHED-UP BUTTER

WHAT YOU NEED:

- **Blender or food mixer with a clean bowl**
- **Measuring jug • 280 ml double cream**
- **Clean kitchen towel • Your pet adult**

WHAT YOU DO:

1 Chill the blender bowl in the fridge for a couple of hours.

2 Pour the cream into the bowl and blend it for a couple of minutes until it turns into thick gloopy whipped cream. Try not to eat it…

BEWARE OF CUTTING!
Blenders have sharp blades. Order your pet adult to set up the blender and wash it afterwards!

MAKE SURE THE LID'S ON THE BLENDER!

3 Continue blending until the mixture turns yellow and splattery.

4 Drain off the watery milky liquid into the jug and carry on blending until no more liquid appears.

YOU SHOULD FIND:

The yellow stuff is butter and the liquid is buttermilk. Wash your hands and wash your butter in cold water. Gently squeeze out the moisture and pat the butter dry with a clean kitchen towel. You can make the buttermilk into a milkshake.

OR FEED IT TO YOUR CAT.

WHAT A WASTE!

HORRIBLE MESS!
Washing the butter is really messy!

THIS IS BECAUSE:

Cream is a mix of water and tiny blobs of fat. Scientists call a mix of solid bits and water a "suspension" but it's nothing to do with suspension bridges or being suspended from school...

When the blender whisks the cream very fast, the blobs of fat splat together until you end up with one big splat of butter. And the water? Well, that's mostly in the buttermilk.

Bet you never knew!

In Ireland and northern Europe people buried butter in bogs to preserve it. The National Museum of Ireland has a 200-year-old cask of butter that looks grey and cheesy — anyone fancy a bit of bog butter on toast?

But talking about horrible food – it's amazing what some people are prepared to scoff. In our first queasy quiz you have to decide whether the person in these true stories actually ate the foul food...

The CURIOUS CHEW-IT-OVER Quiz

1 In 1644 Danish author Theodore Reinking wrote a book supporting his country against Sweden. The Swedes jailed him and gave him the choice of having his head cut off or eating his own book. What happened next?
a) He ate his book.
b) He lost his head.

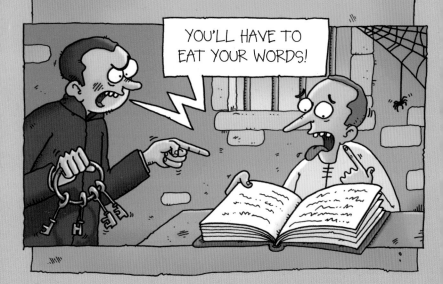

YOU'LL HAVE TO EAT YOUR WORDS!

2 In 1907 German bank-robber Hans Schaarschmidt was locked in a cell with wooden bars. What happened next?
a) He ate the bars.
b) He ate his jailer.

3 In 1939 a student at Harvard College, USA placed a live goldfish in his mouth. What happened next?
a) He let the goldfish swim in his mouth for three days.
b) He swallowed the fish.

4 In 1971 a Swiss couple took their poodle, Rita, to a Hong Kong restaurant. They asked the waiter to feed Rita in the kitchen but there was a misunderstanding and Rita returned on a dish served with a juicy sweet-and-sour sauce and Chinese vegetables. What happened next?
a) They ate the dog and said it was very tasty.
b) They were very upset.

5 In 1994 fisherman Renato Arganza was thrown into the sea off the Philippine Islands. After days in the water he was starving. What happened next?
a) He ate a passing octopus.
b) He ate his underpants.

ONLY IF YOU PROMISE NOT TO LOOK!

Answers:

1 a) He made it into soup. (But don't try this with a Horrible Science book – they're really tasteless!)

2 a) He escaped but was caught three weeks later and thrown in a cell with iron bars. Hmm – I'd have preferred choccie bars!

3 b) He started a stupid craze for swallowing goldfish – the record set in 1974 is 300 live fish.

4 b) Would you eat your pet dog?

5 b) Then he was rescued. I guess he bare–ly escaped with his life.

Vile Vegetables

The second part of your horrible scientist training takes us into the weird world of foul food plants. But be warned – some of them are sure to make you feel a bit green, and the poisonous ones could turn you green for ever!

PUTRID POISON-PLANT SALAD

POISON SALAD? HEY, THAT'S HARD TO SWALLOW!

I'D RATHER YOU DIDN'T TRY, GUTZACHE...

SNIFF

WHAT YOU NEED:
- Salad bowl • Spoon • Two ripe red tomatoes
- Two sticks of celery • Garlic-infused oil
- Chilli-infused oil • Your favourite mayonnaise
- Knife and chopping board • Helpful pet adult

WHAT YOU DO:

1 Wash the tomatoes and celery in tap water.

2 Younger readers should order their pet adult to do the chopping. (Make sure they don't splatter blood over your salad – it does ruin the taste.)

BEWARE OF CUTTING!

3 Place the chopped salad in the bowl and pour chilli and garlic oils over them. Don't use too much – they're strong!

SO I FOUND OUT!

4 Stir well with a spoon.

5 Eat with your favourite mayonnaise. That's if you're brave enough because…

Every plant in your salad contains POISON!!!

YOU SHOULD FIND:

• Celery leaves contain irritating poison that can make your skin sore.

- If you eat tomato leaves or the stem you can end up being violently sick.
- Chilli peppers contain an irritating poison that turns the inside of your stomach bright red – that's why they're so hot.
- Garlic is poisonous to some bugs – it's even used in certain insecticides (that's the posh name for insect-killers).

But actually, you can tuck into this salad in perfect safety…

THIS IS BECAUSE:

- *You're eating the celery stalk and not the leaves.*
- *You're eating tomato fruit (the pips are their seeds) and they're harmless too.*
- *Chilli peppers are poisonous but the amount of poison in each one is tiny. You'd have to gobble over 10 grams of poison in order to die – and no one can eat that much chilli in one go.*
- *Garlic isn't poisonous to humans – although it may have a fatal effect on your social life.*

So why do some plants make poisons? Well, like you, they're not terribly keen on being eaten alive by bugs or beasts. So they produce poisons for protection. Other plants such as tomatoes want animals to eat their fruit in order to spread their seeds in dung – but they don't want their fruit scoffed before the seed is ready. So they make the unripe fruit nasty to eat.

Bet you never knew!

In Roman times people wore crowns of celery leaves (complete with irritating juices) to banquets. Hmm – that sounds a little rash to me!

POTATO
POWER

WHAT YOU NEED:

- A fresh baking potato (not an old mouldy one)
- A plastic drinking straw
- A little brother/sister or a gullible pet adult

GULLIBLE ADULT

EVIL IDEA!

Hmmm...

WHAT YOU DO:

I Bet your little brother/sister/gullible adult that you could cut a hole in a potato without using a knife.

2 Hold your plastic straw like this.

STAB!

POTATO

3 Bring it down on the potato in a single swift movement.

YOU SHOULD FIND:

The straw cuts a hole in the potato and you can collect some easy money!

THANKS, GUTZACHE!

GRRR... I CAN DO THAT!

THIS IS BECAUSE:

The straw is a tube and that's a strong shape. You probably think that a force is when you're FORCED to go to school. But to scientists a "force" is something that moves an object or squashes it out of shape.

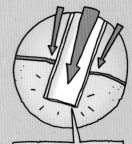

ALL THE FORCE IS CONCENTRATED ON THE END OF THE STRAW

This gives the straw real pushing power and it is enough to spear the spud. It's an easy experiment as long as you don't trip on the cat...

GRRR!

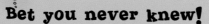

Bet you never knew!

The heavier a moving object is the harder it is stop it with another force. Scientists call this "inertia".
This explains why it takes 1.6 km to stop a supertanker even with its engines blasting in reverse. And it's why trying to stop a cannonball with a tennis racquet is a bit silly.

NOT-SO NASTY NETTLES

WHAT YOU NEED:

- A handful of stinging nettles. Pick only the young nettle-tops and wear gloves and long sleeves for this dangerous job (see warning)
- Your pet adult
- A small onion
- Saucepan
- Wooden spoon
- Olive oil
- Garlic oil
- Flour
- Tablespoon
- A stock cube
- Blender
- Glass with 200 ml milk
- Measuring jug
- Colander
- Knife and chopping board

OK GUTZACHE, I'LL EAT NETTLES IF YOU PICK THEM.

RATHER YOU THAN ME!

WHAT YOU DO:

1 Heat the cooker to a medium heat.

2 Wash the nettles in the colander – but don't touch them!

3 Order your pet adult to chop the onion finely – that way they can do all the crying!

WEEP DRIP

HEY – I WAS THE ONE WHO GOT STUNG!

4 Add two tablespoonfuls of olive oil and one tablespoonful of garlic oil to the saucepan.

5 Place the saucepan on the cooker and gently stir the onions until they're turning brown.

6 Add the nettles and stir them gently with the wooden spoon until they're dark and wilted.

7 Meanwhile, order your adult to boil a kettle of water and make up 300 ml of stock using the instructions on the stock-cube packet.

8 Pour a tablespoon of flour on the nettles and stir well. Then, and this is a bit tricky, add a little stock at a time until the liquid is soaked up in a gooey mass.

9 Add the 200 ml of milk and stir well. Carry on stirring until the soup is simmering and any lumps of flour have dissolved.

BEWARE OF BURNING

Beware hot soup splashes! Younger readers should order their pet adult to do step 10.

10 Order your pet adult to take the soup off the heat and cool it for ten minutes. You can then pour the soup into the blender and liquidise it.

11 Order your adult to reheat the soup. And if you're brave enough you can slurp it up with nice crunchy bread and your homemade butter.

SLURP

AND IT'S REALLY TASTY!

GRRR...

YOU SHOULD FIND:

You can eat the soup *without* getting stung.

THIS IS BECAUSE:

Nettles sting by injecting you with a mix of chemicals that cause soreness. When you touch a nettle you break the tips off tiny hairs. But heating probably breaks up these chemicals so they won't harm you.

SHARP HAIR PIERCES SKIN

GUTZACHE

NETTLE LEAF

CHEMICAL FLOWS INTO BODY

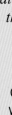

EVIL IDEA!

Hmmm...

Let your friends try your soup but don't tell them they've been eating stinging nettles until after.

Bet you never knew!

A traditional cure for the painful joint disease arthritis involved whipping patients with stinging nettles. Sounds a weedy idea? Well, no — in 2000 British scientists found that stings seemed to help some sufferers. But don't try whipping granny with nettles — you might get a few stinging remarks!

HE! HE!

HE! HE!

SNEAK

CREEP

VEGGIE MUMMIES

I AIN'T SCARED OF VEGGIE MUMMIES!

CALM DOWN GUTZACHE– IT'S ONLY AN EXPERIMENT!

WHAT YOU NEED:

• Half a cucumber • A large flat-bottomed bowl and a smaller flat-bottomed bowl that will fit inside it • Salt • White sugar • 150 ml vinegar • Fork • Jug • Tablespoon • Knife and chopping board • Measuring jug • Your pet adult may be needed for chopping duties • A heavy tin of something – try Watson's dog food

PANT

SLOBBER

NO, I AIN'T FEEDING YOU!

WHAT YOU DO:

1 Wash the cucumber.

2 Use the fork to scratch deep lines in the cucumber's green skin. Just imagine a mummy's long sharp nails scratching human flesh.

I'D RATHER NOT!

3 Slice the cucumber so thinly that you can see daylight through the middle of each slice.

4 Place the cucumber slices in the larger bowl and sprinkle a tablespoon of salt over them. Mix well. Next, place the small bowl on top of the cucumbers. Weight it down with the tin and leave for two hours (this is the boring bit).

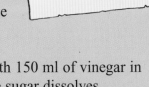

HORRIBLE DANGER!
Beware careless cutting! Younger readers definitely need a pet adult for this job.

5 You'll find that much of the juice has drained out of the cucumbers.

6 Mix a tablespoonful of sugar with 150 ml of vinegar in your jug. Stir the mixture until the sugar dissolves.

7 Pour away the cucumber juice and add the vinegar mix to the cucumber slices. Stir well and leave the slices to chill in the fridge for three hours and then munch them with some tasty chopped parsley.

YOU SHOULD FIND:

The cucumber is dry and crunchy.

THIS IS BECAUSE:

Just like you, a cucumber is made of microscopic living cells. Cells take in water but they lose it if they are surrounded by sugar or salt. The scientific word for water moving in or out of a cell is "osmosis".

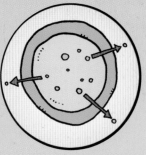

As the cells dry out, it becomes harder for germs to rot the cucumber. This preserves the vegetable.

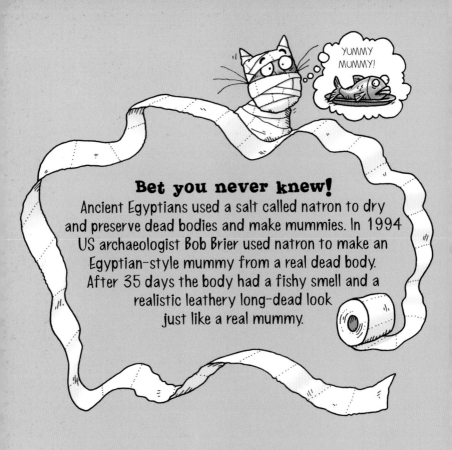

Bet you never knew!

Ancient Egyptians used a salt called natron to dry and preserve dead bodies and make mummies. In 1994 US archaeologist Bob Brier used natron to make an Egyptian-style mummy from a real dead body. After 35 days the body had a fishy smell and a realistic leathery long-dead look just like a real mummy.

Well, it looks like this putrid plant chapter is squelching to its foul finish – but there's just time for a queasy quiz. So can you tell your grapes from your gooseberries?

The PUTRID PLANT Quiz

1 Why wouldn't you want to eat a skunk cabbage?
a) It stinks like a skunk.
b) It tastes like a skunk
c) It's poisonous and it stinks like a skunk.

2 How did the goldfish plant get its name?

a) Goldfish can't resist nibbling it. They even leap out of their bowls and wriggle towards the plant on their bellies. Then they die.
b) It looks like a goldfish.
c) It pongs like a goldfish (a long dead one).

3 What do the rafflesia and the voodoo lily have in common?
a) They would make an ideal gift for your teacher.
b) They stink of rotten meat.
c) They're used to make perfume.

Answers:
1 c)
2 b) Mind you, it doesn't fool many people – after all fish don't normally grow on bushes.
3 b) And if you still think the answer's a) you ought to be expelled.

Extreme Egg-speriments

Horrible scientists find eggs fascinating –
especially smelly eggs and creepy
snake eggs. And you can use eggs
for some especially evil experiments –
as you're about to find out…

FLOATING EGGHEAD

FLOATING EGGHEAD SOUNDS LIKE YOU IN A POOL!

PAT PAT

GRRR!

TUG

WHAT YOU NEED:
• One egg • A large glass • Felt-tipped pen with waterproof ink • Salt • Tablespoon • Measuring jug • Cold water (leave a jug of water in the fridge for an hour or two)

WHAT YOU DO:

1 Measure 250 ml of tap water and pour it into the glass. Then place the egg in the water. As long as it's fresh, the egg should sink (eggs that are going off may float).

2 Remove the egg and stir in 4 tablespoonfuls of salt. Stir well until all the salt dissolves.

3 Dry the egg. Dry the egg and draw a face on the shell.

Draw the face of someone you don't like.

4 Take the jug of cold water and slowly trickle some water on to the salty water. Try not to stir up the salty water.

5 Place the egg in the glass again.

YOU SHOULD FIND:

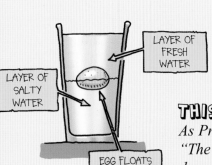

LAYER OF FRESH WATER

LAYER OF SALTY WATER

EGG FLOATS ON TOP OF SALTY WATER

The egg sinks, but NOT to the bottom of the glass.

THIS IS BECAUSE:

As Professor N Large would say, "The egg sank because it's denser than water". Density is the amount of material in an object compared to its size – so a pebble is denser than a beach ball (if you don't believe me try dropping them on your toe). Adding salt to water makes it denser than the egg – so the egg floats on top of the dense layer of salty water. Simple, really!

LOOKS LIKE I'M LESS DENSE THAN YOU!

DUH - ARE YOU CALLING ME STUPID...?

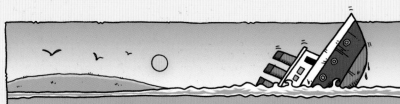

Bet you never knew!

Here's the deal. You sail my overloaded ship. If it sinks you die and I get a big insurance payout. Refuse and you get sent to jail. Sounds unfair? Well, in the 1870s that was the choice for sailors when shipowners overloaded their ships. In dense salty seas the ships were OK, but warmer water wasn't so dense and some ships sank lower until they sank completely. In 1876 politician Samuel Plimsoll backed a law that forced owners to paint a line showing the safe water level on their ships. This lifesaving "Plimsoll line" is still in use.

BOUNCING EGGS

BOUNCING EGGS? YOU'RE KIDDING!

TRY IT AND SEE, GUTZACHE.

WHAT YOU NEED:

- An egg (you can use the egg from the previous experiment complete with silly face)
- 150 ml of white vinegar (cider or white wine vinegar is fine)
- A glass

WHAT YOU DO:

1 Place the egg carefully in the glass – we don't want any breakages now…

2 Pour the vinegar over the egg and watch carefully. The egg is soon covered in tiny bubbles.

3 Leave the egg for 48 hours.

You'll need to turn the egg a few times and place a spoon to keep the egg at the bottom of the glass. (The bubbles make the egg float.)

YOU SHOULD FIND:

The egg feels rubbery because it has no shell. In fact you can even drop it into the sink from 4 or 5 cm and it will bounce…

HEY THAT'S WEIRD!

BOING!

THIS IS BECAUSE:

Eggshell contains calcium carbonate – that's the stuff you call "chalk". Acid in the vinegar dissolves the chalk and releases carbon-dioxide gas (yes, that explains the bubbles). Without a shell to break, the egg bounces if you don't drop it too far…

OOPS, SORRY GUTZACHE!

SPLAT

I WAS JUST GOING TO SAY– **DON'T BREAK THE EGG!** YOU'LL NEED IT FOR THE NEXT EXPERIMENT!

MAKE AN
ALIEN EGG

WHAT YOU NEED:

- **Your bouncing egg from the previous experiment**
- **Tablespoon**
- **A packet of sugar**
- **Two jars**
- **Green food colouring**
- **Plastic drinking straw**

WHAT YOU DO:

1 Place the egg in a jar and pour sugar over it until it is just covered.

2 Leave the egg in the sugar for 36 hours.

3 Now use the straw to add ten drops of green food colouring to a clean jar of water.

HOW MUCH LONGER?

YOU CAN'T HURRY SCIENCE!

4 Gently wash the egg in clean water and place it in the jar for 24 hours.

YOU SHOULD FIND:

After 36 hours in the sugar, the egg feels limp and when you gently touch it, your finger makes a dent. The sugar has turned into a watery syrup. But after 24 hours in the water the egg is firm again. And what's more, it's grown bigger and it's GREEN!

THIS IS BECAUSE:

An egg is a giant cell, just like the cells in the cucumber or the cells that make up your body. A shell stops an egg from losing too much water, but this egg has no shell. When the egg was in the sugar, osmosis (remember that word from page 35?) moved water from the egg into the sugar and left the egg limp. But once the egg was in water it could suck in water and green colouring by osmosis. And because it had no shell it could swell into an alien egg.

The EGGS-CELLENT Quiz

Is there an egghead in your family? Why not test them with this queasy quiz and who knows – they might crack up if they get the answers wrong…

TRUE or FALSE?

1 A "fart egg" is an egg that gives you a bad case of eggy-burps.

2 A double-shell egg is two eggs joined together and laid by the same bird.

3 Some eggs have no shells.

4 A Chinese "century egg" is just that – a 100-year-old egg. People actually eat these stinky old eggs.

5 In 2005 a Chinese hen laid an egg shaped like a spoon.

Answers:

1 FALSE – it's an egg with no yolk. In the past people thought roosters laid these eggs. In fact young hens lay them.

2 FALSE – it's one egg inside the other. The inner egg is often a fart egg.

3 TRUE – they're wrinkled like the egg in your experiment.

4 FALSE – it's a duck's egg preserved for a few months in clay, ash, salt and lime. The egg turns brown and green inside – fancy one on toast?

5 TRUE – the hen lived in Hubei City and woke its owner by making strange noises as it laid the egg. Not surprising really. I've heard of an egg and spoon race but this is ridiculous!

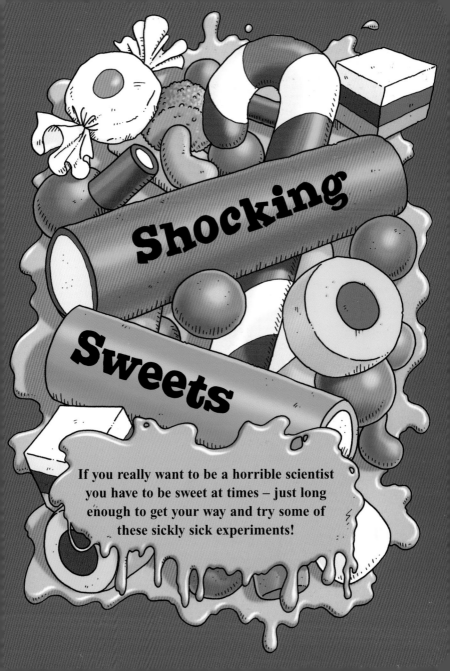

Shocking

Sweets

If you really want to be a horrible scientist you have to be sweet at times – just long enough to get your way and try some of these sickly sick experiments!

SO LONG OLD FRUIT!

WHAT YOU NEED:

- **100 g dried apricots** • **350 ml water (weighing 350 grams)**
- **Two bowls** • **Weighing scales** • **Sieve** • **Measuring jug**
- **Notebook and pencil**

WHAT YOU DO:

1 Weigh the bowls and make a note of their weight. You'll need to subtract the weight of the bowl when you weigh the fruit and water later.

2 Add the water to a bowl and place the apricots in the water. Leave the fruit in the fridge for 24 hours.

3 Pour the apricots and water through a sieve held over the second bowl.

4 Replace the apricots in their original bowl and weigh them.

5 Weigh the water in the second bowl.

YOU SHOULD FIND:

The fruit is about 2.5 times heavier. There's very little water left in the bowl.

THIS IS BECAUSE:

Like any fruit, apricots are made up of cells, and the water has passed into the cells by osmosis. In fact, fresh apricots are mostly water.

Bet you never knew!

For hundreds of years children have been tortured by being force-fed dried plums – otherwise known as prunes. As every granny knows, prunes have a laxative effect on your guts (they make you poo). But scientists have found out that it's not actually the prunes that make you want to go – it's a chemical in the prune juice. That's why prune juice is a laxative too.

OPEN WIDE!

YUCK!

SPIDERS IN JELLY

UGH – YOUR PANTRY IS FULL OF SPIDERS!

I'LL CLEAN IT UP TOMORROW.

THAT'S WHAT HE SAID YESTERDAY...

HORRIBLE DANGER!

Beware cutting and scalding! Younger readers should order their pet adult to do the dangerous jobs such as cutting up jelly and adding boiling water.

WHAT YOU NEED:

- A packet of jelly (any flavour you like – I used strawberry and told everyone it was blood)
- Scissors
- Spoon
- Your pet adult
- Measuring jug
- Kettle
- Heatproof glass bowl
- A toy spider, worm or cockroach (or anything that doesn't float); give the toy bugs a good wash and rinse in clean water

WHAT YOU DO:

1 Order your pet adult to cut out six cubes of jelly and place them in the measuring jug.

2 Younger readers should order their pet adult to risk scalding by pouring 140 ml of boiling water from the kettle over the jelly cubes.

3 Stir the cubes until they disappear completely.

4 Add the same amount (140 ml) of cold water and give the mixture another good stir.

TUM–TE–TUM...

WHAT THE PROF DOESN'T SEE...

5 Now for the interesting bit. Add your bugs to the bowl. It's a good idea to place the bugs against the edge of the bowl so you can see them better. Now pour the jelly mixture over the bugs.

6 Place the bowl in the fridge for 12 hours.

YOU SHOULD FIND:
The jelly has set and the bugs look revolting.

IS THIS SOME KINDA JOKE?

ER, DO YOU WANT SOME JELLY WITH YOUR SPIDER?

THIS IS BECAUSE:
Most jellies contain a substance called gelatine. This is made of protein molecules stuck together in a rubbery mass.

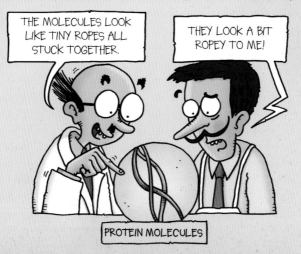

THE MOLECULES LOOK LIKE TINY ROPES ALL STUCK TOGETHER.

THEY LOOK A BIT ROPEY TO ME!

PROTEIN MOLECULES

The hot water loosens the proteins so they float about. When the jelly cools, the proteins link up again, trapping water (and a few revolting bugs) in a big wobbly blob.

HORRIBLE DANGER!

Remove the bugs before allowing little brothers or sisters to guzzle the jelly. They could choke on them!

Bet you never knew!

1 Revolting Roman Emperor Heliogabalus (AD 203–22) served his guests real spiders in jelly together with other disgusting dishes such as ostrich brains and parrot heads. In the end, Helios was murdered on the toilet and his body thrown in a sewer. And that was the end of his time on the throne.

2 Gelatine is made from cattle hooves and pig trotters, together with bones and other body bits that have been dissolved in acid. The protein is actually called collagen and it's the same stuff that makes our skin tight and springy. As people age their skins lose collagen and that's why they go wrinkly.

YOU COULD USE SOME COLLAGEN, PROF!

{{FUME}}

GRRR

EDIBLE GLASS
Yes, it's true!

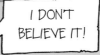

I DON'T BELIEVE IT!

IT'S TRANSPARENTLY OBVIOUS!

WHAT YOU NEED:

- **Flat-bottomed baking dish at least 20 cm by 15 cm**
- **Frying pan**
- **125 g white sugar**
- **Your pet adult**
- **Fish-slice**

WHAT YOU DO:

1 Place the dish in the fridge for two hours.

2 Pour the sugar into the frying pan. Younger readers should order their pet adult to heat and stir the sugar.

The sugar will turn yellow and melt into a gooey brown liquid. The liquid needs to be stirred until all the sugar has melted.

3 Order your pet adult to carefully pour the hot sugary liquid into the baking dish and quickly tilt the dish so that the liquid spreads as widely and thinly as possible.

4 Place the dish in the fridge for one hour to cool.

5 Use the fish-slice to gently lift the "glass" in one piece.

HEY! IT COULD FIX MY WINDOW...

YOU SHOULD FIND:

The liquid has hardened into a see-through substance that looks like glass. And you can eat it!

THIS IS BECAUSE:

In white sugar the molecules are arranged in three-dimensional shapes called crystals. Heating shakes the crystals apart (imagine kids holding hands and jumping about until they have to let go). As they cool the molecules join up, but they're no longer part of crystals. Light can shine through the gaps between the molecules and that makes the "glass" see-through.

The SICKLY SWEET Quiz

Have you got a sweet nature or are you in a sour mood?
Simply match the sweet food with the fact, but be warned
– one food has two facts.

Foods
1 Honey
2 The stevia plant of South America
3 Sugar
4 Sweetbread

Facts
a) It's 250 times sweeter than sugar.
b) This substance isn't sweet.

c) This sweet treat was around at the time of the dinosaurs.
d) In 2000 German doctors used this to heal pus-dripping wounds.
e) This sickly substance can be used to harden roads.

Answers:

1 c) Bees were around 100 million years ago. 1 d) 2 a) Stevia leaves are used in sweeteners. 3 e) makes concrete set more slowly. 4 b) It's made from the pancreas (a digestive gland) of a piglet, calf or llama. Anyone fancy a lumpa llama?

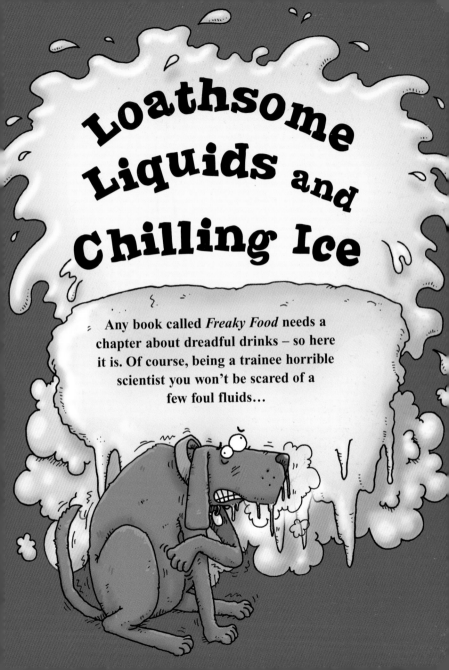

Loathsome Liquids and Chilling Ice

Any book called *Freaky Food* needs a chapter about dreadful drinks – so here it is. Of course, being a trainee horrible scientist you won't be scared of a few foul fluids…

THE FAMOUSLY FOUL COCKTAIL

WHAT YOU NEED:

- A glass
- Measuring jug
- Grapefruit juice (without added sugar)
- Decaffeinated coffee
- Tonic water
- 2 teaspoons
- Glass of water

WHAT YOU DO:

1 Fill the glass with 100 ml of warm water.

2 Add a teaspoonful of decaffeinated coffee.

3 Stir in 100 ml of grapefruit juice.

4 Add 50 ml of tonic water and try just one teaspoonful of the drink.

5 Make a face and spit it out in disgust. Drink some water to clean your mouth out.

SO WHAT'S FOUL? I LOVE COFFEE!

CLANK CLANK

EVIL IDEA!

Hmmm...

Ask your pet adult to sample your cocktail instead. If you're feeling especially evil you could even tell them it's beer and enjoy watching them clutching their throat and gagging...

YOU SHOULD FIND:

The drink tastes disgustingly bitter and I bet your pet adult is feeling a little bitter too...

WHY DIDN'T YOU WARN ME?!

I DID!

WELL, YOU DIDN'T WARN LOUD ENOUGH.

The tonic water is also bitter but it contains sugar to hide the bitter taste. Of course, you may think it still tastes disgusting.

LET'S SEE YOUR TONGUE, GUTZACHE!

Your tongue is covered in tiny bumps – you can see them best on the sides and front of your tongue. The bumps at the back are flatter. All these bumps are called papillae (pap-pill-lee).

They contain taste sensors that detect the molecules that give food flavour. These molecules dissolve in your spit when you eat. Scientists reckon your superb sensors can detect sweet, sour, salty and bitter flavours and umami – a sort of meaty savoury taste.

Your bitter detectors are vital because many poisons taste bitter and you can gag them out more easily.

Fortunately the substances in your cocktail weren't deadly – they just tasted that way!

SUCK SUCK

Bet you never knew!

The bitter taste of coffee and grapefruit is made by a chemical called nurigen. The bitter taste in tonic comes from a medicine called quinine. It was originally added to prevent the deadly disease malaria. Oh well, at least it's good for you.

OILY
SURPRISE

WHAT YOU NEED:

- A glass half-filled with water • Plastic drinking straw
- Green food colouring (or any other revolting colour you fancy)
  • Ruler • Spoon • Cooking oil • Salt

SO WHAT'S THE SURPRISE?

I CAN'T TELL YOU – IT'S A SURPRISE.

GRRR! I'LL GIVE HIM A SURPRISE!

WHAT YOU DO:

1 Use the straw to drip ten drops of food colouring into the water and stir well. Don't add more than ten drops as this will make the water too dark.

2 Pour cooking oil into the water until there is a 0.5-cm layer of oil on top of the water.

3 Lightly sprinkle a spoonful of salt on the oil…

WHERE'S THE SURPRISE?

KEEP WATCHING.

YOU SHOULD FIND:
The salt sinks through the oil to the bottom but blobs of goo start to rise to the surface like bubbles.

HOURS LATER…

THEY'RE NOT FIGHTING.

NOW THAT IS A SURPRISE!

THIS IS BECAUSE:
Oil and water molecules don't mix and oil isn't as dense as water so it floats. As the salt sinks through the oil it drags oil blobs to the bottom. But water dissolves the salt and the oil floats to the surface.

Bet you never knew!
An early car engine ran on peanut oil. The engine, built by the German Otto Company, worked well and I bet it cost peanuts to run. Modern engineers have converted diesel engines to run on waste oil from restaurants – but sadly they don't fry chips at the same time.

LOVELY LEMONADE

WHAT YOU NEED:

- Measuring jug
- Concentrated lemon juice
- Sugar
- Fizzy water
- Weighing scales
- Wooden spoon
- Kettle
- Your pet adult

WHAT YOU DO:

1 Pour 200 ml of lemon juice into the measuring jug.

2 Pour in 180 g of sugar.

3 Younger readers should order their pet adult to boil a kettle and pour 200 ml of hot water over the lemon mixture.

4 Stir well until the sugar dissolves and allow the liquid to cool.

5 When it's cool you can store it in the fridge. You can mix it with fizzy water and serve it to your guests. (The less water you add the sweeter the drink will be – but that's up to you!)

YOU SHOULD FIND:

It's really tasty!

THIS IS BECAUSE:

As you slurp your lemonade you're actually zapping two types of chemical taste detectors in your tongue. There are acid detectors that sample the sour lemons and sugar detectors that give you a nice sweet taste. The sweet taste distracts you from the sour taste and together they taste really refreshing.

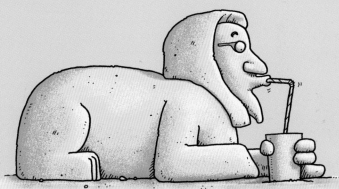

Bet you never knew!

Lemonade might be one of the world's most popular drinks but no one knows who invented it. All that's known is that people were swigging a sugary lemon drink in Egypt 700 years ago. I expect it made a nice change from the daily rind, oops — I mean grind.

INCREDIBLE INSTANT ICE

WHAT YOU NEED:

- A breakfast bowl
- Gloves
- A clean plastic drinking straw
- A bottle of still mineral water (unopened)
- A watch or clock
- Freezer
- Clingfilm
- Tweezers

HORRIBLE DANGER!

Ice from a freezer can burn. Wear gloves for this experiment.

DARN! I'VE RUN OUT OF ICE!

DON'T WORRY, GUTZACHE– I'VE GOT AN INSTANT ANSWER.

WHAT YOU DO:

1 Stretch the clingfilm tightly over the top of the bowl.

2 Open the mineral-water bottle. Place one end of the straw in the mineral water and pinch the other end of the straw together – this will allow you to pick up a drop of water.

3 Place the drop on the clingfilm. Now repeat step 2 to place six more drops on the clingfilm at regular intervals.

CAREFUL NOW, GUTZACHE!

4 Carefully place the bowl with the drops of water in the freezer. Don't let the drops slide off the clingfilm!

5 Leave the bowl in the freezer for 12 minutes. You should find that some or all of the drops haven't frozen.

6 Use a pair of tweezers to scrape a few ice crystals off the side of the freezer. Touch each of the unfrozen drops with a small piece of ice.

YOU SHOULD FIND:

The drops turn into lumps of ice – *instantly!*

THIS IS BECAUSE:

A drop of water can only freeze if there's something like a speck of dust for the water molecules to freeze to. Your mineral-water drops were so clean that most of them didn't contain dust and so freezing couldn't start. Instead the drops became "supercooled" – that is, they became colder than freezing. When you added ice the water could freeze to it very quickly.

The COMPLETELY CHILLY Quiz

So could you tell an iceberg from an ice lolly? Each question has two possible answers but to make it a bit more chilling you lose a point for a wrong answer!

1 If you supercool water to −120°C it...?
a) Actually warms up slightly.
b) Turns thick and gooey like syrup.

2 What are the smallest types of icebergs called?
a) Growlers.
b) Squeakers.

3 How cold is the inside of an iceberg?
a) About as cold as my living room.
b) About as cold as my freezer.

4 What sound do icebergs make when they melt?
a) A bubbling noise like my little brother's bottom in the bath.
b) A fizzing sound – like lemonade.

Answers:

1 b) But don't try to drink it – it's so supercooled it will probably freeze your head into a block of ice.

2 a) They're about the size of a small car and they really do growl!

3 b) They can be −20°C – I hope your penny-pinching parents don't keep your house this cold!

4 b) It's the sound of gas that's been trapped inside the ice for 15,000 years escaping as the ice melts. The gas inside your little brother hasn't been trapped for quite that long.

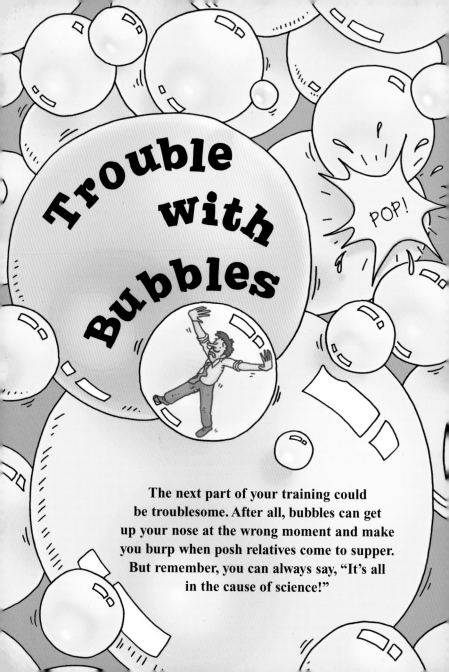

Trouble with Bubbles

The next part of your training could
be troublesome. After all, bubbles can get
up your nose at the wrong moment and make
you burp when posh relatives come to supper.
But remember, you can always say, "It's all
in the cause of science!"

THE LEMONADE DISASTER

M I GUTZACHE IS SHOWING OFF HIS PARTY TRICK...

VÓILA!

I BET YOU CAN'T DO IT WITH LEMONADE.

WHAT YOU NEED:
- **Two identical glasses (6 cm across and 12 cm tall would be an ideal size)**
- **Two identical squares of card or thin plastic (laminated paper or card is ideal). They should be 12 cm by 12 cm**
- **Fizzy lemonade**

WHAT YOU DO:
1 Fill one glass up to the brim with water.

2 Fill the other up to the brim with lemonade.

3 Place one piece of card over each glass.

4 Hold the card firmly over the glass of water. Take it to the sink and…

5 Turn it upside down. Then take your hand away from the card.

6 Now repeat steps 4 and 5 with the lemonade.

HORRIBLE MESS!
If you don't do this over a sink your pet adult might turn a bit vicious!

GRRR!

YOU SHOULD FIND:

The card stays in place even when the glass is upside down. But there's NO way the card will stay in place over the lemonade for more than five seconds.

YOU KNEW THAT WAS GOING TO HAPPEN!

WE ALL DID.

THIS IS BECAUSE:

The lid stays over the water because it's held in place by the force of the air pressing up on it. This force is called (gobsmacked gasps here) "air pressure", and, as you've just found out, this force is stronger than the force of gravity pushing the water on to the card.

Water molecules often "stick" together and the water forms a skin that helps to glue the card to the rim of the glass.

The lemonade won't stay in the glass because the drink contains carbon-dioxide gas bubbles. The gas pushes outwards with enough force to beat air pressure.

GRRR! I'LL GIVE YOU PRESSURE!

Hmm – maybe it's simpler just to DRINK the lemonade?

THE GREAT
BUBBLE MYSTERY

WHAT YOU NEED:

- **Two glasses of the same size and shape (make sure they're clean and dry)**
- **Washing-up liquid**
- **Spoon**
- **A piece of kitchen towel**
- **Lemonade or your favourite fizzy drink**

WHAT YOU DO:

1 Squirt a small blob of washing-up liquid on the kitchen towel and wipe it around the inside of one glass. This glass is glass B – the other glass is A.

2 Fill both glasses two-thirds full with lemonade.

3 Watch what happens in the next few minutes.

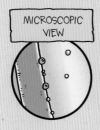

MICROSCOPIC VIEW

YOU SHOULD FIND:

Bubbles appear in glass A. Foam tops the lemonade in glass B but there are few bubbles in the drink. Twenty minutes later glass A is still gently bubbling but glass B is still.

THIS IS BECAUSE:

When you fill the glass with lemonade tiny pockets of air get trapped in microscopic pits in the glass. Carbon-dioxide gas from the drink swells the air pockets into bubbles. But in glass B washing-up liquid molecules pull water molecules into the pits. So there are no air pockets and bubbles can't form.

I'VE GOT MORE BUBBLES THAN YOU!

NOW THEY'RE BOTH COUNTING BUBBLES.

HUMANS CAN BE SO-O-O BORING.

FANTASTIC FIZZING

I DON'T NEED ANY MORE SUGAR. I'M SWEET ENOUGH.

DON'T BET ON IT, GUTZACHE!

WHAT YOU NEED:

- **Glass A and B with lemonade from your last experiment**
- **An identical glass. This is going to be glass C**
- **Three sugar lumps**
- **Food colouring**
- **A clean plastic drinking straw**

WHAT YOU DO:

1 Fill glass C two-thirds full with water to match the level of the lemonade in the other two glasses.

2 Place all three glasses on a windowsill so the light can shine through them.

EVIL IDEA!

Hmmm...

3 Add a drop of food colouring to each glass using the straw. This isn't scientifically vital – it just looks HORRIBLE!

4 Plop a sugar lump in each glass.

ANOTHER WAY TO TEST THE GAS CONTENT OF THE DRINKS IS BY COMPARING THE FIZZ ON YOUR TONGUE... ... BUT DON'T DRINK THEM!

I'M THIRSTY!

GLUG GLUG GLUG

THAT'S THE DRINK WITH THE WASHING-UP LIQUID!

YOU SHOULD FIND:

You'll get a few bubbles in glass C, more bubbles in A and the most bubbles of all in glass B.

THIS IS BECAUSE:

Glass C – water dissolves the sugar lumps and allows air bubbles to escape.
Glass A – there's still a bit of gas in the lemonade. Gas bubbles form around air pockets in the sugar.
Glass B – Bigger bubbles form around air pockets in the sugar because there was more gas left in the drink.

THAT'S WHY THIS CHAPTER IS CALLED BUBBLE TROUBLE.

So did those effervescent* experiments make your brain bubble? Here's your chance to really find out what's between your ears…

Posh word for bubbling.

The BUBBLE TROUBLE Quiz

Match the questions to the answers…

QUESTIONS

1 What kind of bubble can sink a ship?

2 What do you get when you boil a kettle in space?

3 What kind of a bubble surrounds our solar system?

4 Scientists bred yeasts (a kind of microbe) in space. What did the microbes make?

ANSWERS

a) Rather puny bubbles.

b) A vast bubble shaped like a peanut containing scarcely any gas.

c) A giant hot–air bubble.

d) A giant methane–gas bubble.

Answers:

1 **d)** They form from methane on the sea bed.

2 **c)** Bubbles in the water join up inside the kettle.

3 **b)** That's less gas than you normally find in space. The bubble formed when ancient star explosions blew away the gas.

4 **a)** The scientists were brewing beer in space and using yeasts to make the fizzy bubbles and alcohol. The scientists claimed it was an experiment (yeah, right!) but the yeasts didn't breed as well as on Earth. So the beer was a bit flat.

FLAT BEER

SCIENTIST: FLAT OUT AFTER DRINKING BEER

Crucial Clearing Up

Even horrible scientists have to clean up after their experiments – in fact it's a vital part of your training. So let's see how Gutzache and the Professor get on with this challenging task…

STICKY SITUATIONS

WHAT YOU NEED FOR THE GOO PATCHES:

• Orange or lemon squash drink –
it must contain sugar

• A glass • A clean plastic drinking-straw

• Ruler • Pen • Marker pen

• Kitchen paper to mop up sticky spills

• Plastic place mat or laminated card/paper

WHAT YOU NEED FOR THE TESTS:

- **Washing-up liquid**
- **A good friend or pet adult**
- **A watch or clock with a second hand**
- **Three 50p coins and three £1 coins. Try asking your pet adult for the cash**

EVIL IDEA!

If they part with the cash then maybe they'll let you spend the money afterwards!

Hmmm...

GOT SOME CHANGE?

I WANT IT BACK!

WHAT YOU DO:

1 Pour 1 cm of squash into the glass.

2 Use the straw to pick up a drop of the squash and drip it on the place mat or card to make a drop roughly 1.5 cm across. Label this "A".

AND START AGAIN IF YOUR STUPID DOG **LICKS** YOUR EXPERIMENT!

3 Add 1 cm of water to the squash and repeat step 2. Make sure the second drop is the same size as the first one.

If you don't get it right, mop up the drip with kitchen paper and try again. Label the second drip "B".

4 Add another 1 cm of water to the squash and repeat step 2. Label your third drop "C".

5 Leave the drops in a warm place such as a sunny windowsill for 36 hours or until the drops have dried into goo patches.

THE GOO TESTS

6 Now for the exciting bit. Make sure the coins aren't greasy by washing them in water and a little washing-up liquid and drying them carefully.

7 Press a 50p coin onto goo patch C and gently and firmly turn the place mat or card upside down. Your friend should time how long it takes for the coin to drop off.

8 Using another clean 50p, repeat

step 7 for goo patch B. Then use another 50p for goo patch A. If your goo is good at sticking coins in place you may like to test it with the £1 coins.

YOU SHOULD FIND:

Your results may be similar to Gutzache's

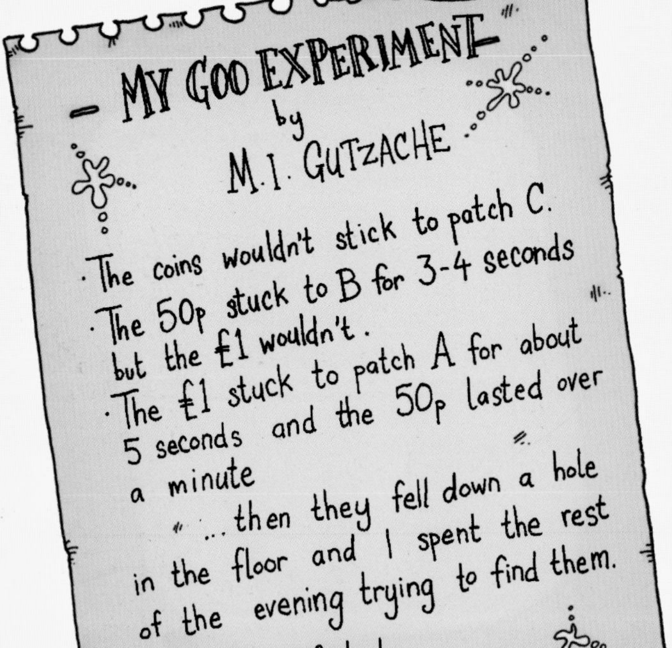

— MY GOO EXPERIMENT —
by
M.I. GUTZACHE

· The coins wouldn't stick to patch C.
· The 50p stuck to B for 3-4 seconds but the £1 wouldn't.
· The £1 stuck to patch A for about 5 seconds and the 50p lasted over a minute

" ...then they fell down a hole in the floor and I spent the rest of the evening trying to find them.

I failed.

THIS IS BECAUSE:

Sugar and water make a sticky mixture. Hydrogen atoms in the sugar and water molecules pull on each other and the more sugar you get in a goo the stickier it is. Goo patch A had the most sugar in it so it was the stickiest.

STICK

SQUIDGE

WOBBLE

Bet you never knew!

In 1919 Boston, USA suffered the ultimate grisly goo disaster. A huge 15-metre tank of molasses (the syrupy gloop left over from sugar-making) broke apart. A giant wave of treacle swallowed up 21 people. No doubt they met a sticky end.

WEIRD WASHING-UP

GRRR! THE PROF MADE ME DO THE WASHING-UP.

WELL, YOU LOST MY MONEY!

- DAILY -
SCIENCE NEWS

WHAT YOU NEED:
- **2–3 drops of food colouring**
- **Plastic drinking straw**
- **Large glass**
- **Measuring jug**
- **Washing-up liquid**

WHAT YOU DO:

1 Fill the glass with 400 ml of warm water from the tap.

2 Use the straw to add 2–3 drops of food colouring to the water (as usual the colouring isn't vital but it looks evil).

3 Allow a small drop of washing-up liquid to drip on to the surface of the water and watch carefully…

BEWARE OF BURNING!

We're not talking BOILING HOT. But be careful – tap water can be hot!

YOU SHOULD FIND:

Weird swirling ghostly patterns appear in the liquid. If you gently swirl the water, the patterns whirl too.

WASHING-UP LIQUID CAN BE FASCINATING!

YOU COULD'VE FOOLED ME.

THIS IS BECAUSE:

Washing-up liquid sinks because it's denser than water. One end of the washing-up liquid molecule mixes with water but the other doesn't – this makes the molecules clump together.

As the drop of washing-up liquid breaks up, clumps of molecules are whirled away by currents in the water to make the patterns you saw.

That's our last experiment, so let's celebrate the end of your horrible scientist training with a foul feast at the Revolting Restaurant...

The QUEASY FOOD Quiz

People eat (and actually enjoy) some very freaky food, but which of the foods on our manky menu are just too freaky to be true?

The REVOLTING RESTAURANT Menu

SICKENING STARTERS

1. Deliciously different sun-dried maggots – chomp on a classic crunchy Chinese snack!
2. Plump, juicy caterpillars and rice from Laos – they're wriggly good!

MOULDY MAIN COURSES

3. Crunchy calf's eyeballs stuffed with mushrooms le traditional French way!
4. Soft and succulent Hawaiian broiled puppy with sweet potatoes.
5. Fresh and frisky Bulgarian bull's tail (you eat it when it's still attached to a live bull!)

DISGUSTING DESSERTS

6. Delicious deep-frozen Siberian mammoth flavoured ice cream.

7. Casu Marzu and biscuits — a lively cheese from Sardinia. It's so lively it's even got LIVE maggots living in it!

Answers:

1 True. 2 True. 3 True — the bits used for seeing are scooped out of the eyeballs. 4 Sorry puppy fans, it's true. 5 False — so don't try biting a bull's bottom! 6 False. 7 True — the worms are actually cheese-fly maggots but this foul food has now been banned.

EPILOGUE
SOMETHING TO CHEW OVER

So you've finally finished this book? CONGRATULATIONS –
you're now a genuine horrible scientist! And that means I can
reveal the shocking truth about science – a truth known only
to horrible scientists... Most people think science is about
brainy boffins in white coats doing mysterious things in labs.
But most people are WRONG!

In fact science is about everything – and that includes you
and the freaky food you eat. And that's what this book is all
about. Just think – even at mealtimes there could be science
sizzling on your dinner plate and science squelching in your
guts... now that really is food for thought!

FOOD FOR THOUGHT? I'VE BEEN POISONED, STUNG AND
FROZEN AND I STILL AIN'T HAD A DECENT MEAL!

WHAT ABOUT ME?

AND ME?

I'M HUNGRY FOR MORE!

GRRRR!!

Enjoyed *Freaky Food Experiments*?
Hungry for more? Then look out for *Famously Foul
Experiments* – it's in the shops now!

ISBN 978 0439 94407 6